DEAR ANORAK

Do you sometimes find that you're in awe of everything?
Look around, and you'll see what I mean.

Take the bicycle for example: isn't it incredible that
a few bits of metal and two wheels can make us glide
so fast? Or the television: it's made of plastic, wires
and glass. But look at what it does! And think of Anorak!
You know that happy mag for kids? Isn't it the best
invention ever invented in the world of inventions ever?

It's undeniable that we are surrounded by the most
amazing stuff; stuff that was invented a long time ago,
even before your granddad was born.
The truth is, we often forget about the origins
of these everyday objects.

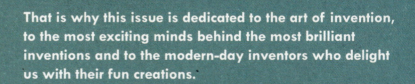

That is why this issue is dedicated to the art of invention,
to the most exciting minds behind the most brilliant
inventions and to the modern-day inventors who delight
us with their fun creations.

I hope this issue inspires you to invent something
extraordinary, like a 'snore-busting' machine for dad,
a doggie-language translation thingamabob or a way
to stop mum from humming so loudly in the streets.
(One can always hope!)

Stay happy!

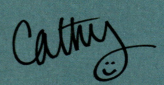
Cathy

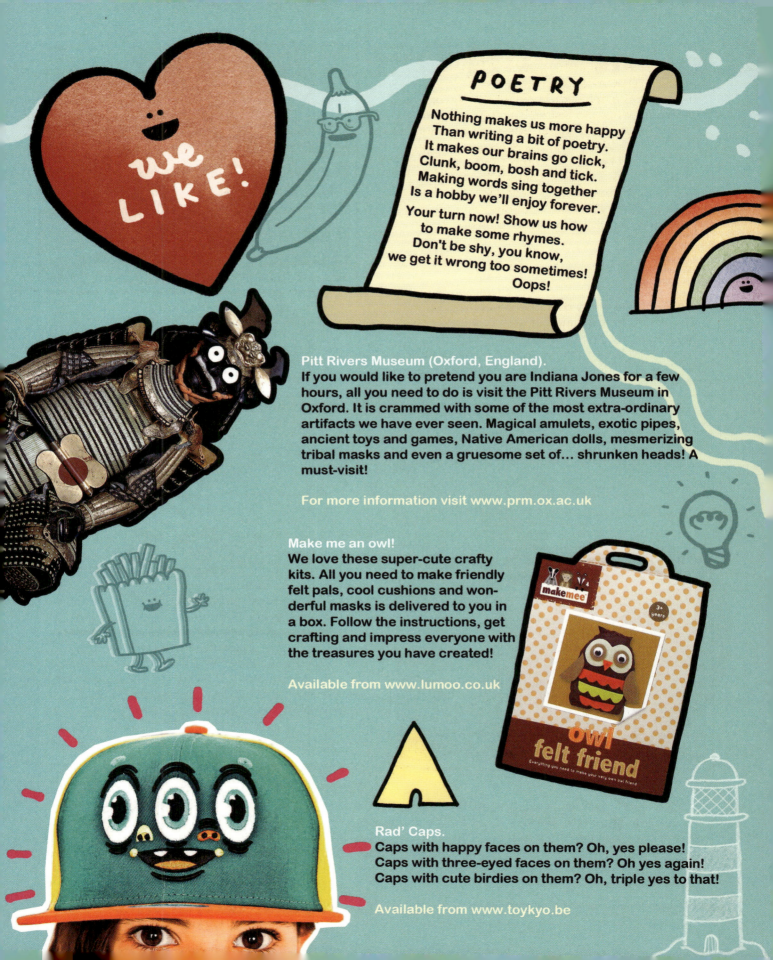

POETRY

Nothing makes us more happy
Than writing a bit of poetry.
It makes our brains go click,
Clunk, boom, bosh and tick.
Making words sing together
Is a hobby we'll enjoy forever.
Your turn now! Show us how
to make some rhymes.
Don't be shy, you know,
we get it wrong too sometimes!
Oops!

we LIKE!

Pitt Rivers Museum (Oxford, England).
If you would like to pretend you are Indiana Jones for a few hours, all you need to do is visit the Pitt Rivers Museum in Oxford. It is crammed with some of the most extra-ordinary artifacts we have ever seen. Magical amulets, exotic pipes, ancient toys and games, Native American dolls, mesmerizing tribal masks and even a gruesome set of… shrunken heads! A must-visit!

For more information visit www.prm.ox.ac.uk

Make me an owl!
We love these super-cute crafty kits. All you need to make friendly felt pals, cool cushions and wonderful masks is delivered to you in a box. Follow the instructions, get crafting and impress everyone with the treasures you have created!

Available from www.lumoo.co.uk

makemee

3+ years

owl felt friend

Everything you need to make your very own owl friend

Rad' Caps.
Caps with happy faces on them? Oh, yes please!
Caps with three-eyed faces on them? Oh yes again!
Caps with cute birdies on them? Oh, triple yes to that!

Available from www.toykyo.be

Tivoli Gardens (Copenhagen, Denmark).
WHEEE! ARGHRGHRGRH!! AHAHAHAH!
OOOH! WOOOAH!
These are the only words we could say for hours and hours when we visited Tivoli Gardens in Copenhagen in the winter. It's such a magical place that it leaves you incapable of forming proper sentences. It houses incredible fair rides, exquisite gardens, an outdoor pantomime theatre, an aquarium, amusement arcades and many many more attractions.
Dear Tivoli, could we move in, please?

For more information, visit www.tivoli.dk

Glowing Pens.
Look at these goofy ghosts! Aren't they funny?
They adorn a new range of mini-highlighting pens that we are currently obsessing over.
Not only do they make colouring in mega dazzling but they also glow in the dark! Too good.

Available from

Tenement Museum (New York, USA).
97 Orchard Street is a building which used to house thousands of immigrants who came to New York during the later part of 19th Century. Nowadays, the apartments (also called *tenements*) have been restored to show us exactly how some of its tenants lived. The Jewish, Irish, German and Italian families who lived there had no toilets or running water. Many fires were accidentally started in the building because people used coal stoves in their small, cramped rooms. It's a great place to visit to remind ourselves how lucky we are now to live in cosy homes!

For more information, visit www.tenement.org

Apples.
We are mad for apples. Green ones, red ones, pink ones; we don't discriminate, we love them all. We love the noise they make when we bite into them. CRUNCH!
We love them in pies. We love them coated in caramel.
Apples, thank you for being one of the best fruits ever.

Available from trees and nice grocery shops.

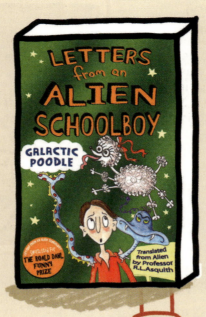

Letters from an Alien Schoolboy: Galactic Poodle
by R.L. Asquith (Piccadilly)

A boy from a distant planet tries to save Earth from aliens with the help of some school friends.
The galactic poodle only appears at the end but I don't want to spoil the story for you. It's quite funny, but not as good as the book before it, which is called Cosmic Custard, so I give it 7 out of 10.
I think boys and girls aged 6 to 8 would enjoy this book.

Alfred (7 years old)

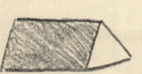

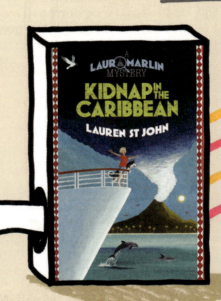

Kidnap in the Caribbean, by Lauren St John (Orion)

An amazing book full of mystery, I have already read it twice.
I love how, just when you think the main character is safe, another awful thing happens! It kept me on the edge of my seat!

Christie (11 years old)

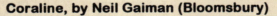

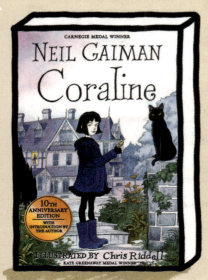

Coraline, by Neil Gaiman (Bloomsbury)

Coraline – or Caroline as she is often called, much to her annoyance – is about 11 years old and small for her age. There is nothing extraordinary about her, she is just a normal girl. But that all changes when she moves into a house with 21 windows and 14 doors. Coraline faces enormous danger and has to be very, very brave. My favourite character is probably the cat. He helps Coraline to think properly and overcome many difficulties. He is exactly how you'd imagine a cat if they could speak.
The story was really interesting and I read the book as fast as possible because I was desperate to know what happened next. The only part of the book I disliked was that it was too short! However, more sensitive people may find the story quite scary; it wasn't full of blood or gore but something wasn't quite right. For that reason, I wouldn't recommend this book to anyone under the age of 10.
Coraline is really gripping and I give it 9.7 out of 10.

Flora (12 years old)

Party Disaster! by Sue Limb (Bloomsbury)

Jess Jordan, a charming but insane teen, decides to throw a small party for her friends and her ex, Fred. But when Jess's party is filled with huge amounts of gatecrashers her house gets trashed. She and her invited guests don't know what to do! This is a hilarious book and I would recommend it to any girl over the age of 10. You will laugh your socks off with Jess and her mates! I really enjoyed this book and give it an 8 out of 10.

Molly (11 years old)

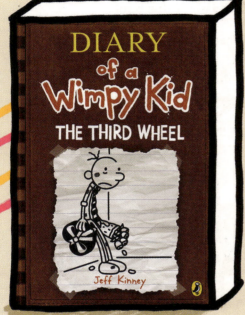

Diary of a Wimpy Kid: The Third Wheel, by Jeff Kinney (Puffin)

It was really, really, really funny. I especially enjoyed the part where Rowley realises that Abigail has a big pimple on her chin and he screams in front of the whole school. This Wimpy Kid book was better than Cabin Fever but Roderick Rules is still the funniest of them all. I would recommend it to kids aged between 7 and 10 years old, because I think that age group will really get it. I give it 9.5 out of 10.

Oscar (10 years old)

A Trip to the Bottom of the World with Mouse, by Frank Viva (Toon)

This book is a very good guide to Antarctica and the journey the author had to get there. I would recommend this book for 3 to 5-year-olds who are interested in the world. Mouse is my favourite character because he is funny. The author lives in Toronto, Canada. He is a cover artist for the New Yorker and the illustrations in the book are great. I rate it 10 out of 10!

Alfie (6 years old)

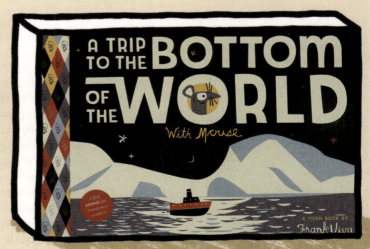

'NEVER SEEN HIM BEFORE, GOVERNOR,' HE BARKED. 'THERE'S ANOTHER MUTT WHO LIVES ABOUT FIVE MILES WEST OF HERE. YOU COULD TRY HER.'

'COME ON,' SAID MUNKIE AS HE MARCHED QUICKLY WEST IN THE HOT MIDDAY SUN. 'WE'VE GOT TO FIND THIS DOG.'

FINALLY THEY REACHED A SMALL BROWN DOG IN A GREEN CAP. 'DOES THIS LITTLE PUPPY BELONG TO YOU?' ASKED MUNKIE.

THE BROWN DOG SHOOK HIS HEAD. 'NO BUT THERE'S A FARM FOUR MILES NORTH OF HERE. TRY THERE.'

ON AND ON THE FRIENDS WALKED. HORRACE AND THE PUPPY WERE TIRED BUT MUNKIE CHEERED THEM ON UNTIL FINALLY THEY REACHED THE FARM.

THERE IN THE FIELD STOOD A BLACK AND WHITE SHEEP DOG.

QUICK AS A FLASH THE LITTLE PUPPY RAN TO HER MOTHER'S SIDE, YELPING WITH EXCITEMENT.

'ALL'S WELL THAT ENDS GOOD,' SAID MUNKIE. 'COME ON HORRACE, I'LL RACE YOU HOME!'

HORRACE ROLLED HIS EYES. 'I THOUGHT YOU DIDN'T LIKE WALKING,' HE SAID.

BUT MUNKIE DIDN'T HEAR. HE WAS TOO FAR AHEAD.

THE END...

ds & picture emma & nathan   thank you molly & clay   shot on great barrier island new zealand   ©rubbishcorp® 2013

Pam & Tom

Words by Cathy Olmedillas   Illustrations by Ben Javens

Pam and Tom are excited. Today, they are going fishing.

Important things to bring on a fishing trip.

A fishing rod

Wriggly worms

A cheese sandwich

A ham sandwich

A sun hat

A rubber ring

A magic wand

How was your day, darling?
Amazing! We caught a whale in less than 20 seconds but we decided to let it go.

How was your day, Tom?
Alright, I suppose. I broke a record for the fastest tree climber ever in the universe.

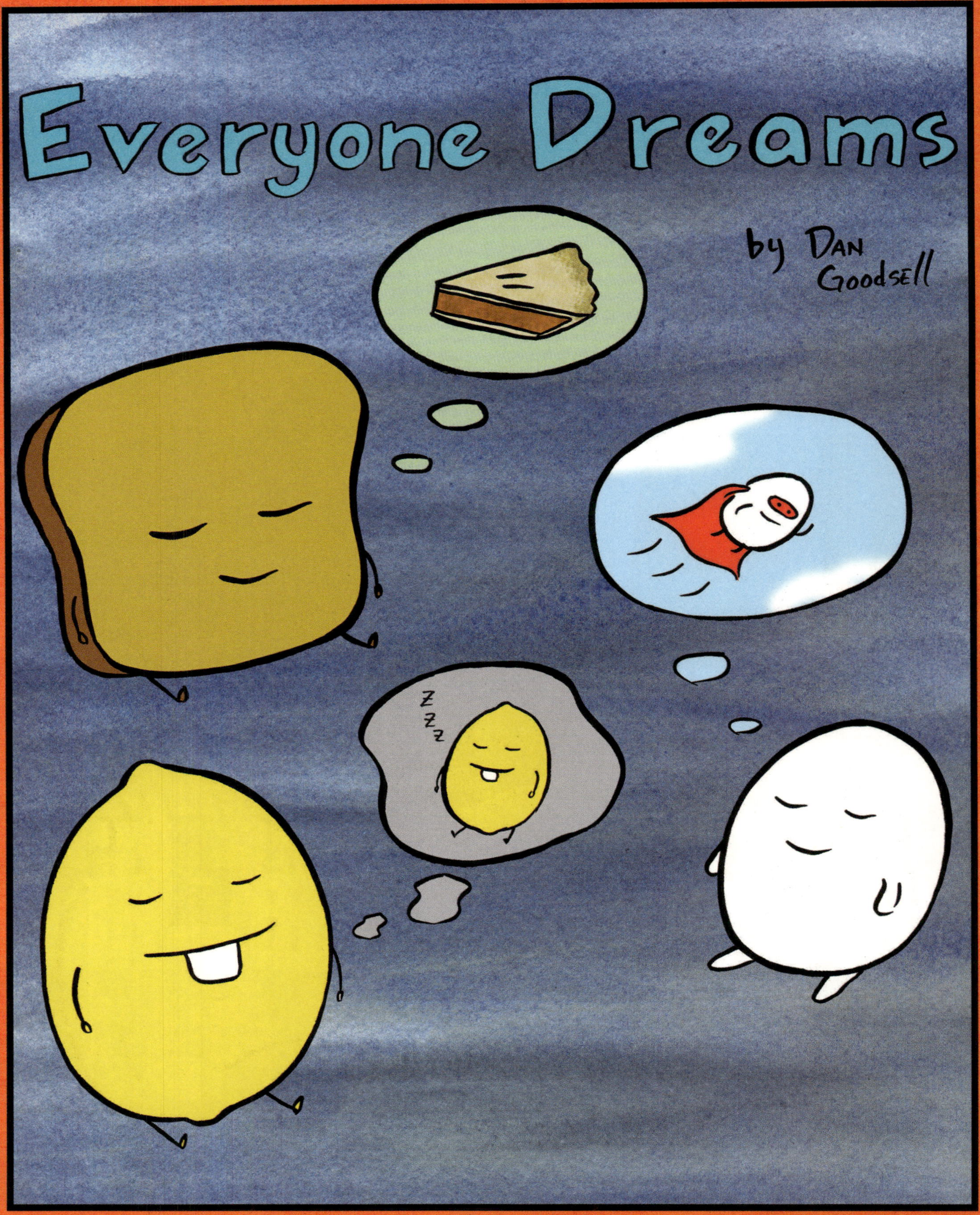
Everyone Dreams
by DAN Goodsell
ZZZ

an alphabestiary

Roy Edwards.

First name in the phone book must be the

aardvark

(Does he wear an aanorak?)

The aardvark aint so 'ard
When confronted by a bruiser,
He tends to drop his guard,
The sure sign of a Loser.

His relative, the Pangolin,
(We call him "The Scaly Anteater")
Is quite good at Slappin' and Stranglin',
But could hardly be called a world beater.

speaking of Anteaters...

The Anteater really has got it all wrong,
For the ant is a very small Snack.
He must hunt them and eat them the whole day Long,
Or his future will Look rather black.

Another Little problem the Eater has with ants,
Although they Look delicious, the taste is rather pants.

For A, i did think Axolotl
Might be fun, but Lost my bottle.

Anaconda

However far you wander
You will find few Anaconda,
For they skulk about by rivers
in the Jungles of Peru.

Now in a fight the victor
Would be the Boa constrictor.
That's why of Anaconda
There are relatively few.

this vark looks more ss•ge than aard.

Hey, what are you doing on this page? off to the next page with you.

No Q jumping! Yes, i know the Pangolin did. Don't answer back!

And speaking of Pangolins....
i just thought of a Pangolin poem. i Liked it so much, i couldn't wait for P. This margin was too wide, anyway....
The Spiny Anteater or Pangolin, is a beast that is best not Left danglin',
For it's tail, though a fine one in so many ways, is scaly and too prone to tanglin'.

The Bee begins with a B
and then there's a couple of EEs.
How busy the Bee must B
Making honey for afternoon Ts.
　　4 a B, U C
can often B
as busy as busy can B.

O.K?

oh Look, here's
a Little swarm
of bs!
They are practicing
for when they beecome
big Bs.

The Bandicoot

The Bandicoot is not a coot
and neither is it bandy.
Apart from that, the name's a "beaut",
apt, pertinent, Jim Dandy.

The Giant Bandicoot's a rat,
it's East and Southeast Asian.
it's hated by the people that
Comprise the population.

it steals their meals and bites their babies,
Squeaks and Squeals and gives them rabies.
Those folks with guns all try to shoot
That wretched, thieving Bandicoot.

Another Bandicoot is Linked
with Central Oz, the Bilby.
it's rare, and though not yet extinct,
It possibly soon will be.

But, though it's neither coot nor bandy,
The Bandicoot has been quite handy.
He's been a Lot of help to me
And filled a space reserved for B.

The Baramundi Perch

Once, I did a Google search
and found the Baramundi Perch.
Just as I thought my search a Failure,
I found it, Living in Australia.

It's the strangest fish that ever was
Put on a china dish because
it always starts Life as a He-male
But in five years becomes a Female.

If you think the old fellow is talking Rot,
Look it up, you'll find he's not.

footnote: animals that change Sex
in midstream are known to biologists
as Protandrous Hermaphrodites.
Not a Lot of people know that.

This footnote is mainly for Geeks
But cool dudes can read it too.

notice board

In the next issue we shall discover how
the Camel got his hump(s) and we'll discover
the Joys of Keeping a Donkey as a pet.
We shall also meet Dolly, my lovely research
assistant......

i Look
forward
to
your
Company

TAP DANCERS

RUNNING WATER

GEMMA CORRELL

Story by Emma Vans-Colina
Illustration by Katie Rewse

The Smallest SCARIEST Spider

Franklin is the smallest spider in the world.
Can you see him? He's up there, right at the end of that sentence.

See? He's really, really small.
If you borrowed Mum's glasses or used a microscope this is what he'd look like.
Pretty nice, huh?

I'm not NICE!

I'm incredibly SCARY!

Every spider wants to be scary — like birds want to fly and fish want to be good swimmers — so every day Franklin practices being more scary.
He brushes up the hair on his legs to make them hairier.
He rolls his eight eyes and bares his tiny fangs.
And when he creeps along the ceiling he does it in an extra creepy way.
The problem is, Franklin is so little that nobody ever notices.

Once, he hid in my sister's lunch box and yelled "Gaaaaah!" when she opened it, but she just took a bite of her apple and Franklin was lucky to jump out of the way in time.

Another morning, he waited at the end of Dad's slipper and tickled his big toe with his hairy legs, but Dad didn't feel a thing.

He even dropped from the ceiling onto Mum's face while she was sleeping, but she just smiled and rolled over.

"I give up!" said Franklin. "I'm a terrible spider. No one will ever take me seriously." And he crept into the corner to be by himself, even though he didn't need to because no one could see him on the wall anyway.

I felt sorry for Franklin. I'd be sad too if I wasn't good at football or writing stories, so that night, at dinner, I explained the situation to my family.

"What spider?" said Dad. "How terrible for him!" said Mum. "Sure we can help," said my sister.

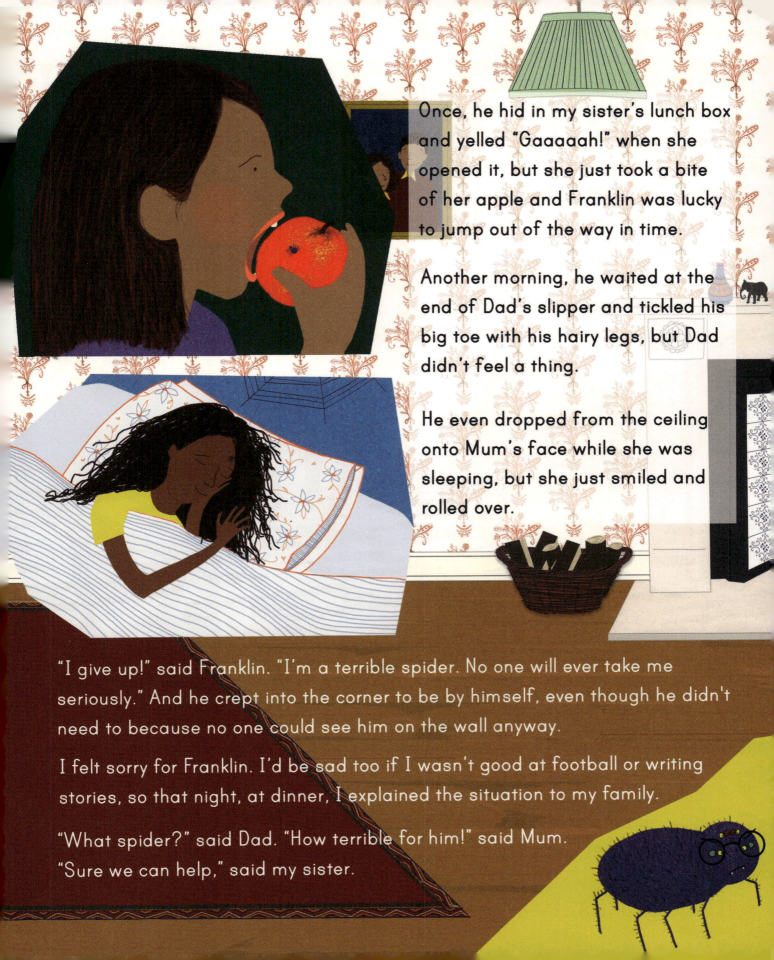

The next morning, when my sister opened the bathroom door, she screamed,

Dad ran into the bathroom and spotted Franklin on the wall near the sink. He jumped up on the toilet and started shaking.

"Arrrgggghhh, a spider! Somebody help!"

"S-S-Somebody get the broom!"

Mum came running with the broom and started swatting it around, all the while being careful not to actually hit Franklin.

Franklin let out a little spider yelp and curled himself up into a microscopic ball.

"I think you've got him," I said, looking around for Franklin.

"Lucky," said Dad, "because that was the scariest spider I've ever seen."

When everyone had gone, Franklin uncurled himself.

"Wow, you were really scary," I said to the tiny spider.
"Yeah, I was," he agreed. "But I was also really scared. I don't think being scary is for me after all."

"Well you're also very nice," I said. "Nice?" said Franklin thinking it over.

The next day my sister found three dead flies in her lunch box for dessert. "Ah, thanks Franklin," she said rolling her eyes. Then Franklin covered Mum and Dad's window with spider webs that glistened like crystals in the morning sun and Mum didn't sweep them away even though they were a bit of a mess. And every night Franklin helps me with my stories, making sure all the dots are where they should be, at the end of every sentence.

The End

NINETY-ONE   NINETY-TWO   NINETY-THREE   NINETY-FOUR

NINETY-FIVE   NINETY-SIX   NINETY-SEVEN

NINETY-EIGHT   NINETY-NINE

ONE-HUNDRED!

A Day Out At The Fashion Museum.

Today, our friends are visiting the world famous Museum of Fashion. They love spotting all the beautiful outfits on display. Join them in colouring its walls and ornaments to make it the most colourful Museum of Fashion ever!

H&M

THE ESSENTIAL ANORAK INVENTING MANUAL

Inventing is easy.

Is it?
It is.
We can all invent something.
All we need is frustration
and imagination.
Everyone has that in them.
"I am annoyed by my homework.
Does that count?"
Err… Yes! If you are thinking
of inventing a 'homework-making'
machine!

Problems are brilliant.

Without a problem to solve,
we wouldn't need to invent
something. The greatest inventors
are those who do not let a problem
stop them. They see a problem
as a reason to create something.

Curiosity is cool. Observing is awesome.

To be a good inventor, you have to want
to know things.
To be willing to find out about things.
To be curious.
It is by observing the world around
us that we are able to find inspiration
to create amazing things. If scientists
hadn't been curious, do you think they would
have built rockets to visit the moon? Exactly.

Imagination is precious.

You too can invent something.
You can invent a word.
You can invent a sound.
All you need is plenty of imagination.
So go on, imagine a new word.
That's it, you are an inventor.

The secret formula of inventions revealed!

30% frustration + 40% imagination
+ 20% determination + 10% sweat
= great invention!

The latest must-have accessories for budding inventors.

An ice pack to put on top of your brain
to stop it from boiling over.
A couple of packets of dreaming gums
to help you daydream and to activate
your brain cells.
A plate full of creativity cabbage
to munch on (fried in a bit of butter is best).
A magical pen that turns ideas into 3D models.
A 'do not disturb' sign on your bedroom door.
A big cup of imagination tea to sip on.

Vote for me! Vote for me!

What is the greatest invention of all time?
You decide.

Humans
Homework
Medicine
Planet earth

VIVA THE VICTORIANS

Since humankind has existed, it has been busy inventing stuff. It seems as though being inventive is one quality humans can't survive without. Imagine being a caveman or a cavewoman and trying to survive without fire or weapons? Precisely.

Throughout the ages, different civilizations have been responsible for amazing inventions, some that we still use today. For example, the Mayans invented bridges, the Chinese paper money, the Mesopotomians astrology, the Greeks democracy and the Olympics.

If there is one period in history where inventing was king, it certainly was the 19th Century. In Great Britain, we call this the Victorian era because it is during that time the mighty Queen Victoria reigned. But it wasn't just in Great Britain where these inventions kept coming. The whole world was gripped by a fever of invention.
Here are some of the wonderful things created back then:

Cameras	Typewriters
Electricity	Radio
Stamps	Penny farthings
Staplers	Electric trains
Sewing machines	The Police
Comic books	Jelly babies
Light bulbs	Flushing toilets
The tube	Paper clips
Ice cream	

And the list goes on!

Draw some of your favourite inventions in the empty boxes.

I INVENTED THAT!

(no, not me, them!)

So, you think that inventions are only devised by bearded men in white coats? That you need to be a scientist or an engineer to create anything clever?

Think again!

Kids are responsible for some of our favourite inventions, and so are ladies. There is no evidence yet that dogs have invented anything (except from lovely furry cuddles), but we think it's only a matter of time!

Take one of our favourite games: Monopoly. Now, you'd be forgiven for attributing its origins to a powerful banker but actually it was a lady who provided the inspiration for Monopoly.
At the beginning of the 1900s, Lizzie Magie created The Landlord's Game, in which players bought and sold land. That concept was later adapted and became the famous Monopoly.

Louis Braille was only 12 years old when he invented a way for visually impaired people to read. He had lost his sight when he was very young but was passionate about reading. So, he set about developing an ingenious alphabet with raised dots, which meant he could feel the letters rather than see them.

A hot day is not a nice day without an ice lolly. Fact. So who should we thank for this yummy invention? None other than 11-year-old Frank Epperson from San Francisco (USA). One night, he famously left a fruit drink outside with a stick in it. In the morning he discovered that it had frozen. To his surprise it tasted quite good. So, 20 years later, he decided to freeze fruit juices on a industrial scale. The ice lolly was born! It tasted so nice that 20 years later he started manufacturing them!

Sometimes, the inventive gene runs in the family. Mrs Josephine Cochran's dad was an inventor and so was her grandad. She was quite wealthy and had many servants to do the chores around the house. She used to get very annoyed with them because while washing her beautiful collection of dishes, they kept breaking them! But what did she do to stop these breakages? She invented the first mechanical dishwasher! We're very thankful to you, dear Mrs Cochran, because washing dishes is BORING!

MEET SOME REAL INVENTORS!

Mark Champkins has a dream job. He is the 'inventor in residence' at the Science Museum in London (England). All he does all day is invent fun things for us to enjoy, such as the brilliant 'pre-chewed pencils' or levitating crockery.

Did you invent things when you were a kid? If so, what did you invent?

Yes. I'm one of three brothers, and my dad encouraged us to make things when we were young. I came up with an idea to make an elastic band gun, which was simply a piece of wood with elastic bands stretched taught with a clothes peg. When you squeeze the peg, it works like a trigger and you can fire the elastic band. My brother and a dozen or so kids in the neighbourhood would have huge battles. It was loads of fun!

What do you think is the greatest invention ever made?

It would be easy to say the Internet or Penicillin, inventions that have had a big impact on the quality of peoples lives, but I'm going to go for the humble bicycle. Their design is so simple and effective. For me, getting my first bike was one of the most exciting things that has ever happened to me, and it offered me the chance to explore.

Which invention are you most proud of and why?

I worked on a set of glasses with liquid-filled lenses, the prescription of which can be altered. The lens works a little like the eye; when you push in more liquid, the surface bends and changes the optics.
The idea is that they can be given out in poor parts of the world, where almost one in three people need sight correction. It would be a cost effective way to help people to see clearly, and would have a profound impact on their lives. I was really proud to have been involved with that project.

What invention do you wish you had invented?

I wish I'd invented Sellotape. It's sooo useful!

MARK CHAMPKINS

pre-chewed pencil

DOMINC WILCOX

If you are a regular Anorak reader, you will know our friend Dominic Wilcox. We simply love his inventions because they have one thing that we cannot live without: humour! Here, he shares with us some of his ingenious ideas, which you can find in his new book Variations on Normal.

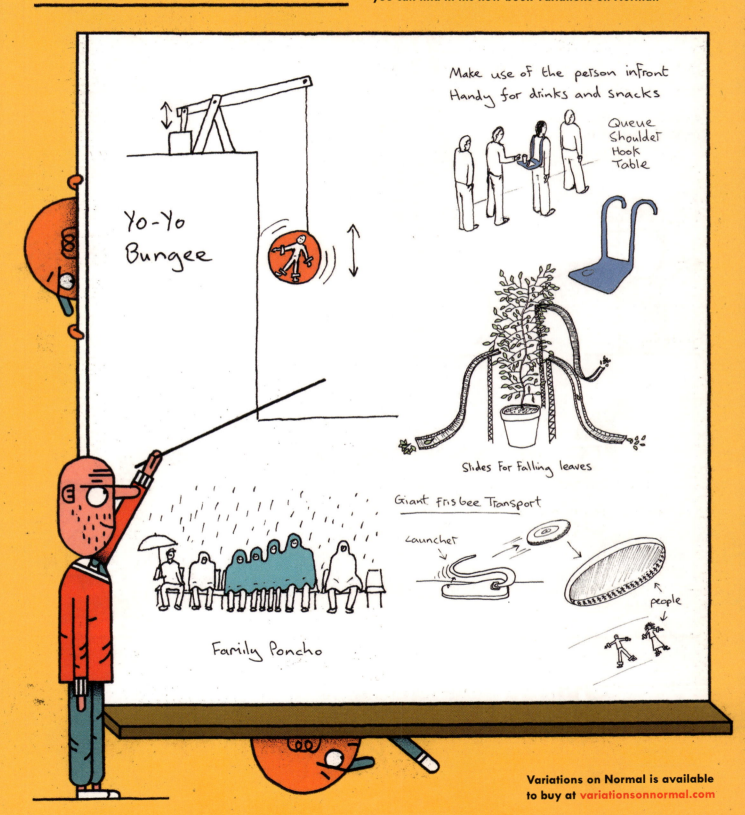

Yo-Yo Bungee

Make use of the person infront Handy for drinks and snacks

Queue Shoulder Hook Table

Slides For Falling leaves

Family Poncho

Giant Frisbee Transport

Launcher

people

Variations on Normal is available to buy at variationsonnormal.com

Hello, I am Peter
and I am a problem.
I love bouncing on this bit
of your brain: the frustration area.
Boing, boing, boing.

Zap! Oh no, who's that?
It's Iris the idea!

Pow!
Ouch!
I have no chance
of surviving Iris!
She is mega fierce
and will wipe me out.

I'd better go and hide
for a while.
I'll be back, though.
When you least expect it.
Mwahahaha.

WHAT IS
THE GREATEST INVENTION
EVER CREATED?

We asked our little editors.
Here are their answers.

"I think wheels are the greatest of all inventions. Wheels are on most kinds of transportation, so that means wheels take you places. When you go somewhere it is an adventure and when you are adventurous it takes you to new places. When you go to new places you meet new people. When you meet new people you learn new things. Learning new things makes you more intelligent and more creative!"
Ava (10 years old)

"Electricity is, as it powers all the other inventions!"
Giuliano (7 years old)

"Doors, because without them, I would not be able to go to my house."
Sarah (6 years old)

"We think the camera was a great invention as it captures the moment."
Zalika and her friend Hannah (12 years old)

"Nail polish."
Madelyn (5 years old)

HELLO!

"Language, because without language, we would not be able to communicate."
William (7 years old)

"I think the greatest invention ever created was pencils and pens! You can draw with them, colour in with them, do whatever you want with them. You can also draw and plan your own creations and inventions. They are so cool!"
Archie (8 years old)

WE COLLECT

Meet Oscar (11 years old).
He loves collecting fun stuff like
key rings, football cards, stickers
and erasers.
In this issue, he shares with us
his amazing collection of Hama
Beads art he has created over
the last four years.

"The first Hama Beads art I ever
did was a lion. That was about four
years ago. Since then, I have
become totally addicted to it.
I now have 94 of them.
Some of them are quite delicate so,
over the years, they have broken.
I must have done well over 100,
if you count the broken ones.
If you have a lazy day at home
and you have nothing to do,
get your Hama Beads out.
It's the most fun to create
all these different patterns.
You can make your favourite
cartoon characters, logos and even
scenes.
Once, I did a logo that was
on my dad's old tennis racket."

"You need a lot of patience. But it makes you happy
because, while you are doing them, in your head,
you think how great they are going to look when
they are finished.
I would recommend that you start with simple patterns.
You don't need to spend tons of money on it.
If you go on eBay, you can buy a few boards and they sell
bags of beads, too. You can look up patterns and ideas
on the internet or even invent your own."

"At first, I was the only one among my friends to do Hama Beads. But then I got them all addicted to them. They come round to mine and we do Hama Beads for a couple of hours.
I have also got my grandparents addicted to them! So you can be from six to 99 years old and love doing them. In fact, if you are over 99 years old, you can still enjoy them."

Do you collect something and would like to see your collection featured in our 'happy mag for kids'? Get in touch via our website!

BEES

The insects' world never ceases to amaze us. If there is one insect that we love, it is bees. We really admire the way they come together to work and how fantastically well organised they are. But let's be honest, we are grateful to them because of the delicious food they produce: yummy honey!

Over the summer, we went to meet Steve Benbow, a beekeeper whose bees make some wonderful honey. Here's what he told us about his buzzy pets.

"My grandmother was a beekeeper, so I guess she is the one who inspired me to start beekeeping. I started about 14 years ago. I didn't have a big garden so I decided to keep them on my roof. I wanted to have a bit of the countryside in London. I bought a nucleus, which is a colony in a box. All of our bees are British, which are a lot darker than other bees.

The weather was very wet last year so we haven't got as much honey as we have had in previous years. Bees love the sunshine but there has to be moisture in the ground because, if it's too dry, there is not much nectar in flowers.

Bees are fascinating. For example, they have two tummies, one for digesting and one for storing nectar. If you see a bee flying around with its legs down, it means its tummy is empty. A queen will live for up to five years but, if she is no good at producing eggs, the other workers will happily get rid of her. Most worker bees live for about a month. In the winter, there are bees that last six months as there is less work to do, apart from keeping the colony warm.

The bees that sting are the guard bees; they defend the colony, you see. They have a poisonous sack. When they sting you, that sack gets ripped apart, which is why they die instantly. Generally, they don't sting and are more scared of you than you should be of them!"

For more information on Steve's bees visit www.thelondonhoneycompany.co.uk or if you are in the USA, we suggest you check the American Beekeeping Federation www.abfnet.org.

Illustration by Evgenia Barinova.

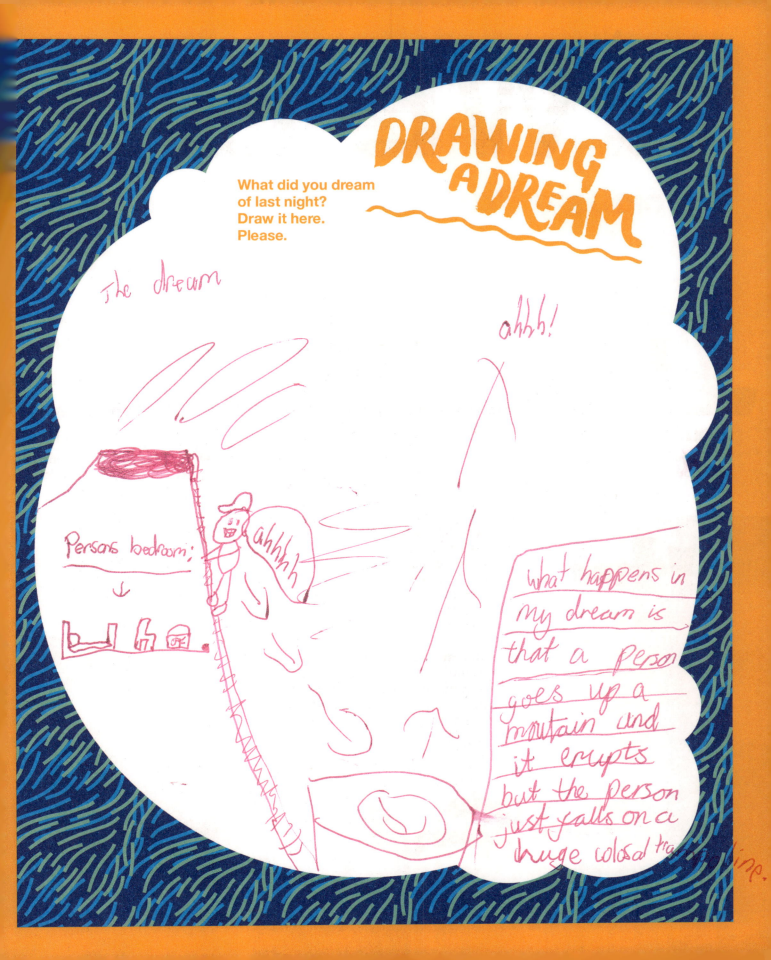

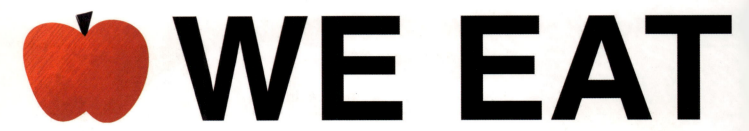

WE EAT

Deliciously Crunchy Toffee Apple Cake!

What you will need:

Flour
1 1/2 cups plain flour.

Butter
300 gr.

Apples
5 pieces. Peeled, cored & sliced into wedges.

Cinnamon
1 tea spoon ground cinnamon (an a little extra for dusting).

Almonds
150 gr. ground almonds.

Eggs 7.

Milk
1/3 cup.

Water
3/4 cup.

Vanilla
1 pod. Seeds scraped out and added.

Sugar
2 1/4 cups.

Baking powder
1 table spoon.

Recipe by Ruth Bruten. Illustrations by Pintachan.

How to make it:

Preheat the oven to 170ºC

Grease and line a 25cm cake tin. It is necessary to line the tin because of the toffee; otherwise all of your lovely cake will be stuck to the tin. Boo hoo.

Place four of the sliced apples over the base and dust a little cinnamon over them. Reserve the other apple to add to the cake batter later.

Place one cup of the sugar and all of the water in a saucepan over a medium heat and stir until the sugar is dissolved. Then STOP stirring and watch the sugar turn golden brown. Magical!

Once the sugar has become golden brown, take off the heat immediately and pour gently over the apples.

In a cake mixer, mix butter and sugar until light and fluffy. If you don't have a cake mixer, just beat the butter and sugar in a bowl. Add the eggs one by one.

Then add the ground almonds, flour and baking powder.

Now, add the eggs, milk, vanilla seeds and a tea spoon of cinnamon.

Turn off the mixer and stir through the remaining apple.

Pour the batter over the toffee-covered apples in the cake tin.

Place in the oven and bake for 30 minutes.

While it's baking, make sure you don't forget to lick the bowl! No point it going to waste, huh? Then cover with baking paper & continue to bake for 45 minutes.

Our deliciously crunchy cake is best eaten slightly warm but will keep in a sealed container in the fridge. Enjoy!

MUSEUM OF CONFUSION

Dylan loves visiting museums. Today he is off to the Museum of Confusion, dedicated to all things weird and wonderful. Could you help Dylan find his way through the museum please?

MUSEUM ENTRANCE

WORM OF WONDER

GIFT SHOP

DUCK OF DELUSION

BEWARE THE ANCIENT KING'S HEAD

TOILET

YOU MUST GO 'ROUND

DARE YOU TRUST THE... LYING HAND?

NO EXIT

MEGA SNAIL OF THE AMAZON!

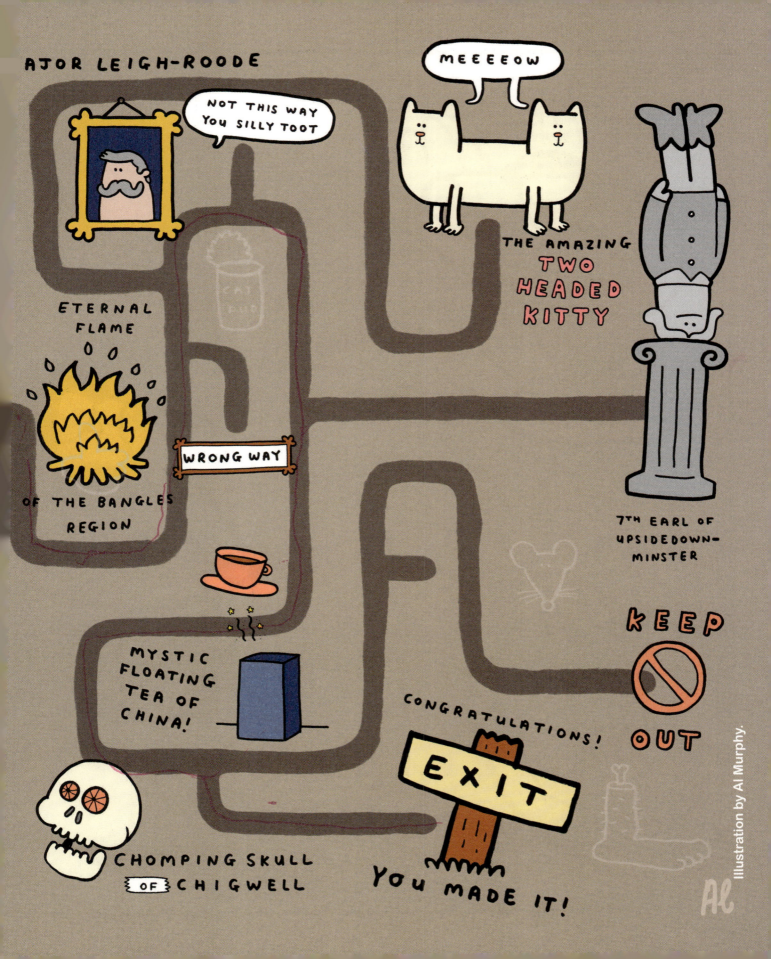

See how many birds you can count in this scene?

Illustration by Leslie Wood.

Answer: six birds.

ANDREW GROVES 2013

LET'S HUNT FOR SOME OF OUR FAVOURITE INVENTIONS!

By Oscar (11 years old)

Anorak
Art
Baths
Board games (one word)
Books

~~Bread~~
Cereal
~~Chocolate~~
Clothes
Couch

Electricity
~~Medicine~~
Santa
Sport
Stationery

~~Teddy~~
Toilet
Toys
~~TV~~
~~Vehicles~~

My name is Laura.
Could you please draw me?

My head is an orange.
My body is an apple.
My arms are bananas.
My eyes are blueberries.
My ears are parsley leaves.
My eyebrows are green beans.
My mouth is an asparagus.

Laura

DRAW ME PLEASE

My name is Christopher.
Could you please draw me?

My head is an hexagon.
My ears are triangles.
My eyes are pentagons.
My arms are rectangles.
My feet are circles.
My mouth is square.

christopher

Rosie Flo's Colouring Page

Add legs, faces and colour in these yummy fashion dresses.

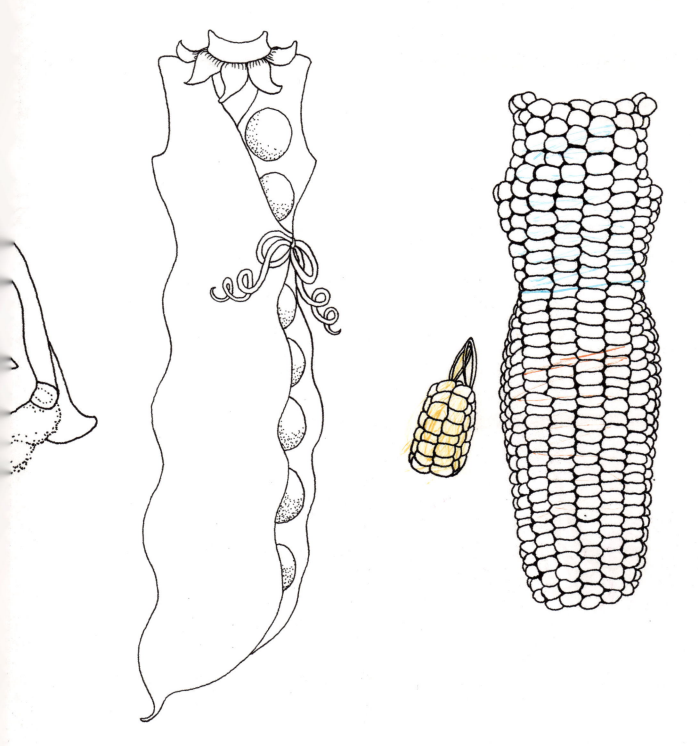

THE TELESCOPE

Words by Marissa Rosenberg. Illustrations by Matthew Bromley

Before telescopes were invented, people thought that the Earth was the centre of the universe and everything, including the Sun, the Moon, and all the stars revolved around us!

They also thought that all objects in the sky were perfectly smooth, perfectly round balls that simply turned around the Earth, and the Earth never moved.

It was only the invention of the telescope that made us realise that not only does the Earth move around the Sun, but the Sun moves around the centre of our galaxy, the Milky Way.

We owe the telescope to a man called Galileo Galilei, who – with it – made three new major discoveries that changed everything we thought we knew about the Universe.

THE MOON

SUN SPOTS

JUPITERS MOONS

The Moon:

It is thanks to the telescope that Galileo discovered that the Moon wasn't all perfectly smooth: it was and still is in fact covered with mountains and craters.

That sparked a new debate: If the Earth was at the centre of everything, how did those craters get on the Moon?

Sun Spots:

Equipped with his new telescope, Galileo found a clever way to look at the Sun safely, without burning his eyes!
He projected its light onto a pale surface.

Similarly to the Moon, it turned out that the Sun didn't look like the perfect smooth sphere that everyone expected.
Not only were there dark spots all over its surface but they were also all different.
Some disappeared, some moved and some suddenly appeared out of nowhere!

This really got people thinking whether their model of the Universe was wrong.

Jupiter's Moons:

If you look at Jupiter in the night sky, it looks like a really bright star. But when you look at it with a telescope you can see it has many different coloured stripes and if you're lucky, you might even see another of Galileo's discoveries: the four biggest, brightest moons of Jupiter, now called the Galilean moons.

People at the time couldn't believe it! They were so sure that everything revolved around the Earth, but if that was true, how can this planet have its own moons that only orbit Jupiter?

With his telescope in hand, Galileo observed these three things, which completely changed our understanding of the Universe. Instead of a Universe with Earth sitting in the middle, as the Sun, Moon, and stars span around us, we realised that we are not at the centre at all!

Earth is just another small part of the vast cosmic playground. This eventually led to the discovery of everything we know about space today.

SPOT THE DIFFERENCE

Illustrated by Tom Hubmann

THERE ARE SIX DIFFERENCES IN THESE TWO SCENES. SEE IF YOU CAN SPOT THEM......

1.Cockerels coombe 2.Marbles 3.Flower 4.Books 5.Bike pedals 6.Jelly beans

ANORAK MAGAZINE
IS THE HAPPY MAG FOR KIDS !

Anorak is published five times a year
by The Anorak Press, part of Oksar Ltd.
Reproduction of editorial is strictly prohibited
without prior permission.
Copyright Oksar Ltd. 2012. All rights reserved.
8 Soda Studios, 268 Kingsland Road,
London E8 4DG.
Anorak™ is a registered
trademark by Oksar Ltd.
Trademark number 2548950.

FOUNDING EDITOR: Cathy Olmedillas
COVER & MAIN FEATURE: Jay Wright
CHIEF DESIGNERS & ILLUSTRATORS: Evgenia Barinova
and Al Murphy
CHIEF SUB: Sorrel Neuss
WRITERS: Nathan & Emma Cooper, Roy Edwards, Ruth Bruten
aka Gourmet Girlfriend, Emma Vans-Colina, Marissa Rosenberg
ILLUSTRATORS, DRAWERS AND DOODLERS:
Dan Goodsell, Gemma Correll, Ben Javens, Katie Rewse,
Dominic Wilcox, Roy Edwards, Maria Cecilie Midttun, Leslie Wood,
Andrew Groves, Pintachan, Matthew Bromley, Adam Higton,
Tom Hubmann, Rosie Flo and Alex Kosowicz.

FSC
www.fsc.org
MIX
Paper from
responsible sources
FSC® C002375

Anorak is printed
on FSC® certified
70% recycled paper,
using biodegradable
vegetable ink.

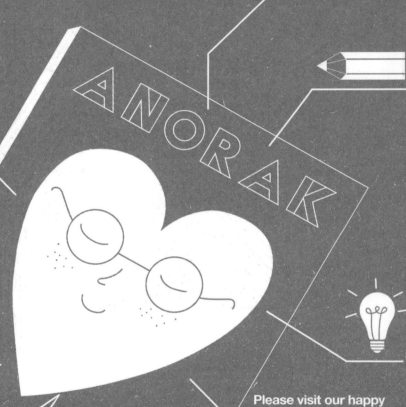

Please visit our happy
website for list of stockists,
subscriptions and other fun!
www.anorakmagazine.com

ANORAK NORTH AMERICA

Anorak North America is co-published
with Gibbs Smith, PO Box 667, Layton,
Utah 84041. It is sold throughout
the USA and Canada.
For more information and subscriptions,
please visit
www.anorakmagazine.com/northamerica

PLOC

PLOC is the happy mag for little ones.
It is aimed at children aged 7 and under.
It carries games, stories, and fun things
to make. It is exclusively illustrated
by the world-famous artist Alain Grée.
For more information about PLOC,
please visit www.anorakmagazine.com